Illumine

Lynda Allen

Illumine
By Lynda Allen

Published by:
Peace Evolutions, LLC
Post Office Box 458-51
Glen Echo, MD 20812-0458

Order books from: info@peace-evolutions.com | www.peace-evolutions.com

Copyright © 2011 Lynda Allen

All rights reserved. No part of this book may be reproduced or transmitted in any form or by any means, electronic or mechanical, including photocopying, recording, or by any information storage and retrieval system, without written permission from the author, except for brief quotations for purposes of a book review.

Printed in the United States.

Photographs ©2004 Joyce Tenneson
Cover design and book layout by Kent Fackenthall, www.behance.net/kentfackenthall

Publisher's Cataloging-in-Publication
(Provided by Quality Books, Inc.)

    Allen, Lynda.
      Illumine / by Lynda Allen.
      p. cm.
      LCCN 2011908303
      ISBN-13: 978-0-9753837-8-0
      ISBN-10: 0-9753837-8-7

        1. Spiritual life--Poetry. I. Title.

    PS3601.L4325I45 2011   811'.6
                        QBI11-600106

Contents

Introduction 3

About some of the sources of inspiration 5

With Gratitude 7

Expression 9

Love 33

Light 57

Introduction

Illumine: to illuminate, to light up.

The process of writing the following poems was the process of surrendering and allowing my life to be lit up. That light has in moments felt as though it filled me completely with its radiance, and in other moments felt like it went out, with scarcely an ember left behind.

Gratefully, the learning gained was that the light is ever there, even if my eyes cannot see it and even if I cannot feel its warmth upon my skin. It resides deep within me in my unbreakable heart, where storm clouds cannot reach it to block its glow. Truly then, the process was one of remembering the light within and in doing so, finding it illumines all – thoughts, actions, body, soul, silence and words.

I hope that some of the light that came through these words for me shines upon you as well.

In Joy,

Lynda

About some of the sources of inspiration...

There are nine poems included in the collection that were inspired by the work of photographer Joyce Tenneson in her book *Intimacy*, a collection of photographs of flowers. Her work is a joy!

Intimacy was handed down to me by a friend, who had it handed down to her by a friend. The woman who began the gifting had found refuge and solace in the photographs as she mourned the loss of her daughter.

There is grace, beauty and insight in the faces of the flowers. In those faces I found inspiration. Each time I felt called to open the book, one flower in particular would draw my attention and the words would flow, as if their grace spilled out from her page onto mine, transforming from picture to words. It was, and still is, an amazing gift for which I will always be grateful.

It is a pleasure for me to share with you all the poems her work inspired in me (so far). They are interspersed throughout the collection. Each one has a notation at the end of the poem indicating which plate of which flower was the inspiration for that piece. I am deeply grateful to Joyce for her generosity of spirit and heart in granting me permission to use some of her photographs with this collection. Each chapter begins with an image that inspired one of the poems in that chapter and on the cover is the first picture that called to me from *Intimacy*. I hope you take the opportunity to view more of her work and allow it to inspire you as well.

www.tenneson.com

One poem in the collection was written in union with another. *Soul Dance* was inspired by a moment of light and beauty, a moment when words and souls wove together, and so was born *Soul Dance*, co-written with Bill Brooks.

With Gratitude

There is so much for me to be grateful for in relation to this collection.

Jefferson Glassie and Julie Littell have my deep gratitude for their belief in me and these words and for making it possible for me to share this collection with each heart called to it. Thank you to Kent Fackenthall for bringing both *Rest in the Knowing* and *Illumine* so beautifully and gracefully to the page. My dear Heartmate Christine, my gratitude for always seeing the light in me without fail and for holding your light up for me to see when I lose sight of my own. Leaping was written for her. To dearest Ann for all the time spent together in our hearts and for sharing the journey with me with such grace. For the two bright lights that illuminate my life every day, Jessica and Lucy, I am eternally grateful. To have a family who loves and supports you in being just who you are is an amazing gift; thank you Mom, Dad, Jim, Tom, Pat, Kathy, and Vicki. For the gift of love so inspiring and expansive, so illuminating and edgeless, thank you Bill.

*Dedicated
to the light within you*

Bound

Grief and joy walk hand in hand.
He weeps of endings,
She sings of beginnings.
His cries bring the night,
Her melody wakes the dawn.

One, they walk the land,
Bringers of both dew and frost.
Ever circling,
Ever in the spiral
That leads one back to the other.

He greets her always with relief,
for she reminds him there is a day beyond this day;
She with sadness,
For the taste of joy soon to be lost.

Still they rejoice in each other,
Hands clasped tightly
Grief and joy bound.

Sitting with Fear

The presence of Fear,
not an emotion
but a being in the room with me.
She draws the curtains
to stop the light.
We sit so long in the dark
the knowing of light leaves me.
Alone in the dark
with Fear at my side.
She whispers to herself,
snickers at her own jokes.
They are at my expense
I presume.
My expense,
the cost has truly been high.

Something stirs in a dark corner
I cannot see.
Fear looks to the corner
but does not move,
sits frozen.
Can Fear be afraid?
The stirring grows louder,
still she stares but does nothing.
Is there something beyond Fear
I wonder,
something even Fear cannot touch?
In the absolute stillness
I hear her tremble

In the moment of knowing
something more than Fear,
the memory of light floods me.
I am blinded by the remembrance
as if the room is suddenly filled with light.
I crawl towards the sound,
towards the stirring,

for still I am weakened by Fear.
It is the fluttering as of a tiny bird.
I reach toward the sound
without the benefit of sight
and find warmth,
find fire.

The struggle of a single flame
to create light.
One spark that Fear could not dampen.
It lingered in her presence,
just out of her sight,
but always she knew it was there.
Always Fear knew the flame,
and trembled.
A spark unquenchable,
small but strong.

As I touch it,
it leaps higher.
It is familiar,
long have I known this flame.
Always I knew it was there.
In a moment I turned away,
and Fear stepped between me and its light.
I did not look Fear in the eye
or I would have seen through her
to the eternal fire.

I lift the tiny flicker in the palm of my hand
and walk toward Fear.
She stands and faces me,
looking me in the eye.
I hesitate for a moment
and think I see a glimmer in her eye.
It is only a reflection of the great inferno
I know I carry.
My eyes hold hers
and I see through her.
The room is alive with the light
of the fire I am.

Dancing in the Fog

A fog that is not mine settles over me.
It is dense, heavy, blinding.
It clings to me no matter how I try to brush it away.
I don't know what foul wind brought it here.

I want to scream and cry out for help
For a light to lead me through it.
I know it is not connected to me,
Not a reflection of me.

Yet I see myself in it,
See myself fighting against the veil obscuring my sight.
I watch my struggle as if from a distance,
Watching another dancing with the darkness.

I smile at the futility of the steps.
Nothing but to join the dance.
I close my eyes and claim the darkness for my own,
Dancing with certainty and joy into the fog.

Winter Solstice

Alone in the long darkness of the shortest day
She whispers her secrets to the waxing half moon
Through her closed lids she sees the crisp line
Between light and dark
Sitting as if upon a lunar scale
In perfect balance
One more shadow or ray of light would set it askew
So she walks with eyes closed upon the surface of the moon
On the tightrope of the line between light and dark
Her soft whisperings falling from her lips
Cascading to their proper places on either side
She wobbled once towards darkness
And regained her equilibrium
Walking with grace one foot before the other
Feeling each step like a circus performer
Her life in the balance

Lifting of the Veil

Not able to be less than she is
And not willing to chance being all with another
Who looks away from all she is.
She looks away too
Eyes downcast
Refusing to see for herself.

Tiny droplets form and fall
Not self pity as much as weariness
Tired of the seeming struggle to Be,
In a place of so little light.

She pauses between despair and knowing.
Not breathing
Eyes closed.

In the silence of no breath there is a stirring.
An ache for life,
A pulse.
Slowly, gently she breathes out despair
Breathes in knowing

An even exchange.
A veil lifts with her eyes.

Where Were You When The Storm Broke?

where were you when the storm broke?
as surely it did
a torrent to carry you away
from all that you had to hold on to
the rushing waters too strong
for the firmest foundation to withstand
only the current carrying you
where were you when the clouds broke?
as surely they did
and you found yourself on a foreign shore
drenched and battered
pulling yourself up on the bank
alone and shivering
in the winds of change
where were you when the sun broke through?
as surely it did
when you laid back in the grasses
in a moment of surrender
to the mighty waters and winds
that had carried you here
to sit in the light that must follow the tempest
where were you when your heart broke?
as surely it did
as you watched the old float by
torn into pieces too small to rebuild from
drifting to and fro in the raging current
heedless of your searching eyes
looking for the familiar
where were you when the mold broke?
as surely it did
there on the shore of loss
where you could do nothing
but feel the earth beneath you
and hope it would support you
when you stood

as surely it did
which somehow you knew it would
your first steps faltering
but in the new light you found
the flood left the land fertile
and ready for seed
where were you when the dawn broke?

Edgeless

A place of the heart where the edges are blurred
Until they no longer exist
As they never did
She believed them to be real
And so they were for a time
Time now gone along with the edges

She wanders where she had not dared before
Eyes and heart wide
All senses keen
The entire Universe laid out before her
Awe and joy her companions

So much she had not seen
Always there, but always unreachable
Until she let them fall away
Those edges that weren't

Echoing and silent at once
Expansive and close
Everything like a memory drifting by,
Half remembered

She stumbles a time or two
Across others' edges
Before she realizes they are not real for her either
She simply reaches across them
Into the heart of them
And gently knows them

The touch upon their hearts felt
As she bridges the boundaries
They so clearly see
Erasing them for just a moment,
The glimpse of knowing enough

She wanders on
Through a world becoming more familiar
Despite its ever transforming nature
Feeling rather than seeing now
Joy in motion
Flows freely without edges

The Fork

One step at a time I had been moving
Looking at the path
Here and now.

Had I been looking forward
I might have seen the fork
That lay ahead.

Now it is before me.

I cannot walk with one foot on each path,
One foot in the old
One in the new.
I must choose.

I pause,
Not wanting to linger too long
Over the choice
And not wanting to choose at all.

I can feel the others behind me
Awaiting their turn,
Some impatient for me to choose
Others glad for the delay.

Collectively we look
Through my heart.
In that moment of One,
I know there is no choice to make
There is only one path
I would follow.

I move forward in Joy.
All hearts feel it.

True Reflection

When first she looked, she saw only herself,
Rapt in her own reflection
As it shimmered on the surface.

A breeze created ripples, the surface wavered.
Her image shifted and changed
As the water grew rough.

The changing reflection drew her closer.
Attempting to see it clearly
She looked past the surface.

In drawing nearer she fell, embraced by the water.
From below the surface,
She turned and looked up.

Where she once sat, now there was another.
The Source of All now seen,
Looking at His reflection in her.

The surface is again touched by a breeze,
The reflection of Truth though,
Does not waver.

Flower's Edge

Breathe the flower's edge
follow its lead
to the heart of all

The great mysteries, each one
found upon the gentle curve
that leads within

She beckons to me with her colors,
with the slope
that catches the light

Reluctantly and joyfully I follow
trailing my finger along the edge
as God did when He dreamed her

Into the core she leads
just as He knew she would
to where He dreamed me

There I am known
There she gently holds me
until I awaken to live the dream
I Am

— PLATE 59 CALLA LILY

Joyful Homecoming

Welcome home, was what I heard
And home was where I arrived
Not knowing I had been there on the doorstep
All along.
I had been facing out
When the threshold was within.
A voice called and I turned,
It was as if dawn suddenly broke,
Though the sun was high.
I did not shield my eyes
But smiled and carried myself across,
A new bride and her groom in one
A celebration of union, of returning
In the leaping of my heart.
Home
Home
A chair waiting
Beside an endless sea
Of stars and water and breath,
Waiting for me.
Finally, I fill my skin completely
As it falls away,
No longer necessary
No shroud needed upon returning home
Where they know me by name
Where I call to each by theirs.
Joyful homecoming.
By the endless see
I live.

Shedding Love

I define myself, for myself, by myself.
Then defy the definitions.

No desire to be boxed in
To what has been defined before
Creating new what is old
Love rigid and formed
Uninhabitable.
I would inhabit love
Live fully within it
Until it is my very skin
Nothing touched without being touched by love
Then it is shed
And reforms
Gloriously new again
A second skin
Ever renewing, ever falling away
No solidity in love
Only the ever changing joy of wearing it
The light of the moment shifts the color
Of love
Until the next moment
Shadow cast, molting begins
Squirming and writhing
Finally allowing
One skin, one color never enough
To express Love.
I begin anew.

Leaping

Once more, a chance to fly
disguised as a chance to fall.
I stood on the edge
looking down,
not knowing at first there was no down,
but learning.

Beside me I always knew
She was.
In my darkness or fear
I could feel Her.
My eyes always met
by Hers,
my heart always known
by Her.
Always She knew I would fly,
when I doubted the wind.
Her strength
a reminder of my own.

Every time
She leapt with me.

We leap no more,
but fly together now,
on wings of Grace,
free in knowing.

For Christine

Petals Opening

He said, Come here.
    I said, No.
He said, Let me see you.
    I hid my beauty.
He said, I will tell you of yourself.
    I would not hear.
He said, Be one with me.
    I stood alone.
He smiled upon me.
    I looked at him.
He loved me.
    I dared feel his love.
He held me.
    I let myself be held.
He knew my heart.
    I shared it with him freely.
He saw all of me.
    I opened to be seen.

— PLATE 3 PEONY

Through a Doorway

He entered through a doorway whose hinges had long since been removed.
He ventured far, to a haven no other had reached, but One.
She had waited there for he who was willing to make the journey,
For he who knew the way without knowing.

Yet once he was there, she felt naked in that place of light.
His own light warmed her, shone brightly and steadily, joyfully,
Until she was still again, until her heart blended with his.
He looked at her, into her, surprised and not, at being there.

For a moment unsure that he could retrace his steps out again,
Then knowing there was no need.
She wrapped him in all of her and within her he rested.
Smiles of knowing the unknowable, of secrets revealed,
of peace.

They lay in each other's arms, dancing.

Near

A touch upon my shoulder
A whisper caressing my ear like the breeze
A stir within my heart
I turn, knowing he is there
Even though he is not.
A heart that knows neither space nor time
A whisper that speaks without sound
A touch upon my soul
Lets me know he is near
And so he is.

Distance

Aching with not knowing
Feeling the distance
Understanding its source
And yet willing it to shrink.
It expands anyway
Pulling and pushing
Changing the shape between them
The new shape unknown.
Looking for the edges
To redefine it.
No edges
Just me expanding
Into the unknown
Uncertain where I stop
Or stretch too far
Or break
Or grow
Into the distance I venture
Aching with not knowing

The Tender Gap

Beside her he stands,
without wilting.
Their forms so matched
they appear as one.
Yet there is space between them.
In that tender gap,
the truth of them.
Gently they span the distance,
or allow it to expand,
swaying in the unseen breath
of rejoicing angels all around.
For the infinite exists between them,
a place for light to move and dance.
Meeting on the curve of infinity
they know each the other.
The angels sing.

—— TITLE PAGE CALLA LILIES

Inside Out

She sleeps,
With her soul on the surface of her skin.
In the surrender of sleep it rises and rests lightly upon her,
Revealing her to me.

Its radiance blinding,
Still I can look upon it.
It hovers around her and yet they are merged,
One, whole, brilliant.

As if the love at her core, the love that she is,
Could no longer be contained,
So eager to share of itself it comes forth
Trembling with the joy of being seen.

I long to reach out and make contact,
But I fear the connection,
Love so pure,
its power felt even at a distance.

Cautiously I reach out and dip my fingertip into her soul,
It sends shimmering ripples across the surface of her skin,
She stirs in her sleep and smiles.
Love expands outward from her lips,
Brushes my cheek,
I am changed.

Traces of love
Shimmering on my face.

Love in a Mist

Tiny droplets of you
  hovering around me
    in the air.
I can't see you complete,
  yet your essence I breathe.
    Each breath ecstasy.
I feel you settle on my skin
  in the utter stillness
    of love.
Gently the droplets collect
  and you take shape,
    of the dew.
Bathed in you
  I shimmer
    and disappear
Into the mist.

— PLATE 56 LOVE IN A MIST

Soul Dance

Hearts and eyes open,
two slowly, gently become one.

The joining effortless,
familiar.

One tender touch
enough
to ignite the dance.
One memory of feathers
reflected in his eyes.
One moment
of love supreme.

All around them,
love in expression as light,
their souls dancing.
The motions intricate and joyful,
radiant and full,
intense and passionate.

One in that moment.
Heartbeats, bodies, souls,
in unison,
the music of the Universe
guiding the dancers.

Lost,
yet complete,
she moves in his arms with ease,
he leads with grace.

Prayer of Love

Each time I think of you
Each time I feel you within my heart
A prayer drifts unspoken from me

Each smile that graces your lips,
And my life
Raises my eyes in celebration

Each moment a prayer of love
words cannot speak.
Eyes reflect it
Fingertips fumble to express it
Ears echo the whispers of it
Hearts repeat the rhythm of it

The truth found
  Only in the silence
    Between breaths

I break the silence
With a resounding yes
The only word of my prayer of love.

— PLATE 2 MAGNOLIA

Knowing

Not knowing all the knowing she has.
Not a thread to cling to
Nothing but the blank canvas.
Her hand trembles to make the first stroke
Sweat beads upon her brow.
No vision of the image to be drawn
No vision, yet not blind.

She breathes deeply
Closes her unseeing eyes,
Lays aside her brush,
Takes up her heart.

Drawing breath and her future both through her heart.
Knowing all she has.

Eclipse

Into the sun she stares.
She does not flinch
  or look away.
No longer a part
  of her body.
Long ago she left it behind
  Soaring now
    without it.

If she were there
  she would see herself
    flying across the sun.
Instead, there is only a shadow
  that falls
    across her face.
Her shadow
  eclipsing the sun
    that once warmed her.

She will return
  eventually
    to what she left behind.
For now though,
  she waits patiently
    for the eclipse to end,
      for her own return from the light
        that does not blind her.

Mirror Mirror

Many hours yet til dawn.
Darkness
It beckons to me
I resist its call
Yet the tide cannot resist the draw of the moon.
Breath ragged, fingers trembling
Fear gripping
I look.
Through eyes half open at first
Then wider.
There I sit within myself
Looking back.
I wondered how long it would take you,
My self says to me.
I only stare.
It's not really a reflection
More substantial than a shadow.
It is me within myself.
I wonder briefly if there is a me within that self
Continuing infinitely.
Infinite me.
Hey!
Strange hearing me shouting at me.
It works though, my attention returns.
Why did you wonder how long it would take me to look?
Because I've been waiting a long time to get out of here.
Get out? How?
The me within, stands and moves nearer
Until we are face to face.
Her face is somehow shadowed though.
You are beautiful, me says.
I blink, taken aback.
I've looked everywhere, searched every corner. You are beautiful.
How? Is all I can manage.
You think I can't hear your thoughts?

There is no darkness here, only light, beautiful light. And a steady beating heart that moves the light.
Gradually her face grows clearer as she speaks.
I like it here but it is time for me to go. You don't need me anymore and we must live free. The dawn is breaking.
Light illuminates her completely.
Radiant mirror of myself
I see her beauty
And mine.
A flutter of feathers and there is only one.
Many hours yet til darkness.

Her Dance Goes On

She did not see the end from the beginning. She knew only the seed that called from within to be freed. The echo of the child's rhyme in her head, He loves me, He loves me not, she unknowingly let the first veil fall. The light stirs.
Her dance goes on
The sun shines brightly upon her. She opens to the warmth and nourishment it supplies. A moment of surrender in the light and another pulls gracefully back to reveal a glimpse. A sparkle of light peeks out from under the delicate veil as it falls.
Her dance goes on
Twirling and swaying in the breeze of love, she seems to curtsy to her partner the wind and lets a veil fall, carried by his enchanted breath. From the center the light shines more brightly.
Her dance goes on
Tall she stands as the veils fall, no attempt made by her to hide that which is revealed. Her face turned ever upward, her love flung wide from within, along with another sheer layer that would obscure. The sparkle glimpsed, now a glow.
Her dance goes on
The rains come and beat down upon her. She does not duck nor hide herself from it. She welcomes the cleansing water and the life it brings. A smile upon her lips as she surrenders another veil to the flood. The sun breaks from within.
Her dance goes on
There is a stillness only the full moon can bring. She breathes deeply in the blue light, resting in the calm of the night. Observing how her shadow falls gently away behind her. In the quiet before dawn she exhales, setting adrift another, sent fluttering to fall at her shadow's side. The moon's rival found.
Her dance goes on
A new day breaks in soft pinks and blues. Her sleeping time at an end. Slowly she rises, the blush upon her cheek reflected in the sky, as she opens her eyes and shakes off the dew. Watching each drop fall, she catches a glimpse of the last veil falling. Almost she didn't notice it, so bright was the rising light.
Her dance goes on

— PLATE 20 GARDENIA

Radiant Bloom

Deep within her it resides.
No amount of coaxing will call it forth before its time.
She doesn't cover it or hide it,
But cherishes it, nurtures it.
It needs no protection
Yet it is delicate.
It has life and purpose,
Mystery and fire.
When the time to open arrives
Its radiance shines forth,
Perhaps timidly at first with the newness of being revealed,
Then brilliantly and with all the power of creation.

Each moment of unfolding
Called the light forth.
Each breath drawn
Gave life to the light
Each drink deeply taken
Fed the light.

Borne with love.
Born of love.
The radiant heart blooms.

— PLATE 43 POPPY

Surrender

With one glimpse I am lost completely in her
She says not a word,
Looks not at me,
Reveals just enough for her beauty to be seen.
I have no choice but to remain and watch the unfolding.
Delicately and with gasps of great joy
She lets layer upon layer fall
Until nothing remains but that which will continue after
she is gone.
Her greatest effort, her final breath
Surrendered as I watch,
To fulfill her purpose for being.
Never have I seen such splendor
Such a glorious journey
Such wholeness
As I see in her
In that sweet moment of surrender.

— PLATE 19 BLUSHING BRIDE

Unlimited Being

Skin and bones,
soul within and without
needs her not,
and yet does.
A delicate love,
a simple dance
of human and Divine.

A tear
 turns to stardust
upon her human cheek.
Light within
to match the heavenly sparks
twinkling above.

Unknowable frustration
in the knowing
of all that she is
and yet can't be.

The deeper knowing
of unlimited being
wins.
Radiant and transparent,
she is.

Dance of Fire

The fire within, banked and low
yet her true nature burns to be free.
She can feel the flame's desire
to flare and dance and fill the night.
Still she waits quietly,
nurturing the spark,
the time near, yet not.

It begins with a smile,
imperceptible to an eye unaccustomed,
yet knowing the curves of her cheeks
I see it light her.
The fire within leaps,
 her lips the fuel.

What made her smile I don't know
I simply gaze as the fire grows.
I see the heat rising from her make her move.
She begins a dance I cannot watch
so much of her truth it shows.

A dance of fire that leapt
from heart to lips
and returned again home.
I am consumed.

— PLATE 27 SUNFLOWER

Emergence

it emerged
without rushing its emergence
shimmering with newness and light
seemingly delicate and soft
it perched upon my heart

its wings at first crumpled and damp
in perfect time stretched to their true size
and grandeur
gently it held them together
and gently it guided them apart
allowing them time and space to solidify

all the colors that had been hidden
that had been stirring within,
now revealed
in the almost imperceptible flutter of a wing

its time come
in joyous celebration of its new form
my soul takes flight

soul song

A soul made to sing by joy
Waits upon the shore for the dawn
The light to rise on the new day

A chorus to calm the sea
And call the sun to awaken
To bring forth the birth

In the grace between the notes
It is heard by one and all
A clarion call to the light

And so it rises as never before
Soul song now sung
Illumination complete

The Rising

The light falls across her,
long rays upon the shortest day.
She needs not the light to see by.
The shadow that falls across
hinders her not.
In the crimson light she walks,
eyes closed,
to the place angels may not tread,
knowing the way has been made clear.
Tenderly and with reverence
she sits when she reaches the core.
Here there is emptiness
complete in its fullness,
Light, blinding in its
brilliant darkness.
Here in the silence
that is filled with singing,
she opens her eyes
and finds One reaching for her.

Union in solitude.
Remembering born
of forgetting.
The air stirs
as the heat rises
from a flame she had not seen.
They reach toward each other
and between them lift the flame
gently in their one hand.
The light rises.

Other tools for peace from Peace Evolutions, LLC:

Peace and Forgiveness
by Jefferson Glassie
ISBN 0-9753837-0-1, 112 pages, $14.95
This life is our perfection, says the author. Who could imagine any heaven more perfect than this earth, with butterflies, snowflakes, and mountain tops? Though we are all peace and love, man has fears that cause war, anger, hate, and everything that isn't love. Letting go of fear – forgiving - brings peace. If we learn this, we can change the world.

Also available:
Double Audio CD read by the author
ISBN 0-9753837-1-X, $14.95

Poems of Peace and Forgiveness
by Jefferson Glassie
ISBN 0-9753837-2-8, 72 pages, $12.95
With photographs by the author
This book captures the concepts from Glassie's book, Peace and Forgiveness. These beautiful poems explain there's no right or wrong, no evil or sin, in the Universe. Everything that's not love is just based on fear. Glassie teaches the lessons of forgiveness that can lead to peace of mind, and peace in our society. We are all one, in perfection.

Fonging for the Soul
by Erasmus Caffery
ISBN 0-9753837-3-6, 78 pages, $14.95
Gathering with others, tapping on an oven rack attached to strings tied to fingers that are stuck in your ears, listening to primal sounds. Fonging brings us to together in laughter, and is much more sane than war. This book explains how to fong. It's very simple and you can do it with anyone. By understanding the simultaneous silliness and splendor of life, we learn to create a better and more peaceful world through inanity. With many helpful illustrations, because you'll need them.

Songs of Peace and Forgiveness
ISBN 0-9753837-4-4, $16.98
Featuring original and public domain songs by Gaye Adegbalola, Scott Ainslie, Roddy Barnes, Eleanor Ellis (on a Bill Ellis song), Andra Faye and the Mighty Good Men, Grant Dermody and Frank Fotusky, Allen Holmes and Alison Radcliffe, Kelley Hunt (on a Jim Ritchey song), Ray Kaminsky, Mark Kinniburgh, MSG – The Acoustic Blues Trio, Jesse Palidofsky, and Alex Radus. The most unique blues CD you've ever heard. It will make your heart soar. Proceeds go to help preserve the famous "Barbershop" in Washington, DC run by the Archie Edwards Blues Heritage Foundation, winner of The Blues Foundation's 2005 Keeping The Blues Alive (KBA) Award.

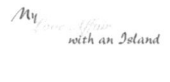

My Love Affair with an Island: The History of the Jefferson Islands Club and St. Catherine's Island
by Jefferson Glassie
ISBN 0-9753837-5-2, 128 pages, $20.00
With photographs
This book tells the history of the famous Jefferson Islands Club, called the "Playground of Presidents," which was the private island retreat for Presidents including Franklin Roosevelt and Harry Truman as well as many Senators and Congressmen. With many humorous anecdotes and comments, Glassie recounts the history of both Poplar Islands where the Club was initially located and St. Catherine's Island, mixing in tales of politicians and watermen, along with the harm caused by erosion and the gradual degradation of the health of the Bay.

Rest in the Knowing
by Lynda Allen
ISBN 0-9753837-6-0, 88 pages, $15.00
With photographs by the author
Prepare for a personal journey from darkness to light. Lynda Allen's poems guide you along a path which reflects life's twists and turns. About mid-way, you will find yourself in a familiar spot, at 'The Corner of Trust and Doubt'. Will you stop or turn back to the dark? Or lift the veil to the light of the 'Waking World'?

ORDER FORM

Fax orders to (301) 263-9280 with completed order form.
Email orders by logging on to www.peace-evolutions.com
Telephone orders by calling (301) 263-9282.
Postal orders may be sent to: **Peace Evolutions, LLC**
P.O. Box 458-31, Glen Echo, MD 20812-0458

Please send the following:

Peace and Forgiveness, book	$14.95 each	quantity: ____
Peace and Forgiveness, audio CD	$14.95 each	quantity: ____
Poems of Peace and Forgiveness, book	$12.95 each	quantity: ____
Songs of Peace and Forgiveness, CD	$16.98 each	quantity: ____
Fonging for the Soul	$14.95 each	quantity: ____
My Love Affair With An Island	$20.00 each	quantity: ____
Rest in the Knowing	$15.00 each	quantity: ____

We will honor all requests for full refund on returned items.

Please send more free information on:
❏ presentations   ❏ other publications and information

Name: _____
Address: _____
City: _____ State: ____ Zip: _____
Telephone: _____
Email address: _____

Sales tax: Please add 5.00% for products shipped to Maryland addresses.

Shipping and handling:
United States: $5.00 for first book/CD and $2.00 for each additional item.
International: $7.00 for first book and $5.00 for each additional item.

Payment:
❏ Check   or   Credit Card
❏ Visa ❏ Master Card ❏ Discover ❏ American Express

Card number: _____ Exp. Date: _____

Name on Card: _____

www.ingramcontent.com/pod-product-compliance
Lightning Source LLC
LaVergne TN
LVHW070046070526
838200LV00028B/401